GRETA'S
STORY

GRETA'S
STORY

THE SCHOOLGIRL WHO
WENT ON STRIKE TO
SAVE THE PLANET

VALENTINA CAMERINI
MORENO GIOVANNONI (TRANS.)

SIMON & SCHUSTER

First published in Great Britain in 2019 by Simon & Schuster UK Ltd
A CBS COMPANY

First published in Italy in 2019 by DeA Planeta Libri s.r.l.

5 7 9 10 8 6 4

Simon & Schuster UK Ltd
1st Floor, 222 Gray's Inn Road
London WC1X 8HB

www.simonandschuster.co.uk

Simon & Schuster Australia, Sydney
Simon & Schuster India, New Delhi

A CIP catalogue record for this book is available from the British Library.

PB ISBN 978-1-4711-9065-0
eBook ISBN 978-1-4711-9066-7

Printed and bound by CPI Group (UK) Ltd, Croydon, CR0 4YY

MIX
Paper from
responsible sources
FSC® C020471

Contents

GRETA THUNBERG

is 15 years old and has an idea: things need to change in order to save the environment. In just a few months, she manages to involve millions of people, ordinary and powerful, in doing just that, drawing everyone's attention to the health of our planet.

With her courage and determination, Greta showed that all of us can do something practical to tackle even the toughest issues. Or, as she herself said: "You are never too small to make a difference."

1

One August morning in Stockholm, Sweden, Greta Thunberg decided she could no longer ignore the problems facing the planet. Changes to the climate were more and more worrying and it seemed as if no-one was taking the problem seriously.

In parliaments all over the world, tens of thousands of serious-looking and stern-sounding politicians sat and talked about an endless range of issues. But they never addressed the problem of the health of the planet. It was time for someone to remind them to step in to protect the environment – and the future of children all over the world. It was an emergency. Everything else could wait.

So, on that day, Greta tied her long hair into two plaits, put on a checked shirt and a blue coat, and walked out of the house where she lived with her parents. Under her arm she carried a wooden placard. Handwritten at the top were the words "SKOLSTREJK FÖR KLIMATET" ("School Strike for the Climate"). She had also made some leaflets to distribute, with some very important information about climate change that she thought everyone should know about.

That day, Greta, like all Swedish children her age, should have gone to school. In Sweden the holidays end in August and classes start again. Instead, she climbed on her bike and rode to the parliament building in the city centre.

The Swedish Parliament meets in a beautiful, serious-looking building that is large and imposing, on a small island with a long, complicated name in the middle of the city: Helgeandsholmen. It's not at all surprising that it's on an island, because Stockholm is built on thousands of islands, some of them tiny and others so big that if you were flying over them you would think they were the mainland.

The Riksdag, which is what the Swedes call it, is the place where politicians elected by the people sit and discuss the country's problems and pass laws to address and fix them. These are the people who can really make a difference. If they hadn't noticed that global warming had become an emergency, Greta would remind them.

Of course, in our daily life, every single one of us can commit to reducing our impact on the health of the planet by limiting waste and pollution as much as possible. But unfortunately, this is not enough. We need more than the good intentions of individual people. Faced with an issue as complex as this, you have to change the rules and make new laws to protect the environment. Who else can do this if not the men and women sitting in the parliament? That's why Greta went there that morning.

On that day – Monday the 20th of August 2018 – Greta launched her school strike.

This is how she explained her thinking: "Children won't do what you tell them to do, but they *will* follow your example." Because the adults didn't seem at all concerned about the future, she was prepared to take action. She would stop going to school. She would go on strike, like the "grown-ups" do when they protest for their own reasons. Instead of going to work, they decide to meet in city squares and in the streets, carrying placards and banners. The difference was that Greta was on her own and was protesting for everyone's benefit.

People passing by looked at the girl with the placard and were curious about her. Perhaps they wondered who she was and what she was doing. She sat there for the time she would normally have been in class, from 8.30 in the morning until three in the afternoon. On the first day, she spent all that time by herself and none of the politicians walking past took any notice. But Greta wasn't discouraged.

The next morning, she got up early, dressed, climbed on her bike and went back to the parliament, again carrying her sign. The strike continued.

But on this second day, something incredible happened: instead of just glancing at her, wondering what she was doing there, and then walking straight past, a few of the people passing by decided to stop. Greta was no longer alone. Other boys and girls joined her.

By the third day, there was a nice little group of people sitting on the ground with her. They were mostly young, but there was also a mother

with a little boy in a stroller, a woman with grey hair and a student who had brought along a book to read. The protesters chatted among themselves. The last few days of that Swedish summer were still sunny.

On the sixth day of the strike, Greta suggested to everyone that they should talk about the protest on their social networks, sharing photos and information. That way, even people who couldn't join the protesters would be able to show their support with a message, a like or a share. The news about what was going on began to spread. Of course, Greta played a big part. Every day she took photos of the *skolstrejk*, the school strike, keeping a diary on Instagram. Friends, schoolmates and acquaintances started asking for information: *can we come too? what time will we meet you?* Greta said everyone was welcome.

More and more people sat with her in front of the parliament building. They were on strike and had decided they would be late for work or school, would skip breakfast at their local cafe or not do their shopping. Day after day, the group of concerned citizens who had decided to follow her example and join the protest, confident that she was absolutely right, got bigger and bigger. They had to act to save the planet, as soon as possible and without delay.

The politicians walked past Greta on the way to their offices in the Riksdag. Although most of them continued to ignore her, occasionally someone would stop to congratulate her and tell her she was doing a great job.

Around the city, people started talking about Greta, the 15-year-old with plaits. Newspaper reporters turned up, as well as some people who were just curious, and others who wanted to show their support. More and more mothers came along with their children. There were grandparents and lots of young people. Someone brought Greta something to eat and drink.

After nine days, the protest was still

continuing but the protesters had to move to Mynttorget, a lovely square on the island of Gamla Stan, in the city's historic centre. It wasn't too far from the parliament, so it was okay. Greta wanted to protest, not break the law.

Meanwhile, all over the world, people were more and more interested in what was happening in Stockholm, and a major English newspaper decided to tell Greta's story. The famous paper *The Guardian* published an online article about the *skolstrejk för klimatet*. The headline read, "The Swedish 15-year-old who's cutting class to fight the climate crisis".

Lots of people were reading about the climate strike in newspapers and thought it was a good idea. Swedes living in other big cities and small towns, from one end of Sweden to the other, heard Greta's call and organised the same kind of protest.

In Linköping, a small town in the south of

the country, a group of people gathered in the town centre next to a fountain and held up a placard that was just like Greta's. A photograph of a bicycle arrived from Rome. Resting against the bike's pedals was a sign that read: "THANKS GRETA! WE'RE ON YOUR SIDE TOO!"

Since that morning in August when she left her house for the first time, headed for the parliament, Greta had a clear goal in mind. She would strike until the 7th of September, which was election day, when Swedish citizens would be voting for their representatives, the men and women who would sit in the parliament.

Because so many people appeared to support her, it seemed a good idea to let as many of them as possible know about the climate strike. Leaflets were distributed inviting everyone to take part in the last day of the protest. They read:

CLIMATE STRIKE!
WHERE? IN MYNTTORGET!
WHEN?
FRIDAY 7 SEPTEMBER!
FROM 8AM UNTIL 3PM
BRING SOMETHING
TO EAT AND DRINK
AND A MAT TO SIT ON.

On the 6th of September, summer was almost over and a grey sky seemed to promise rain. Greta put on her yellow raincoat and on her Instagram profile she wrote to the world that her actions were a cry for help. What she was asking for was reasonable: a future on planet earth. Everyone was invited to take part.

On the following day, the 7th, dozens of people responded to her appeal. Greta had drawn the attention of journalists, politicians and ordinary people to the issue.

Greta reminded the crowd of people who turned up that, among other things, greenhouse gas emissions definitely needed to be limited to stop global warming from making life on earth impossible. So why didn't the candidates up for election make fixing this problem a priority? Why, in

SKOLSTREJK
FÖR
KLIMATET

the weeks leading up to the election, was the environment not discussed?

On her Instagram profile, Greta posted a graph that showed the amount these dangerous gases had to be reduced by to stop global warming becoming irreversible.

What were the politicians doing about this?

Thanks to the *skolstrejk för klimatet*, Greta's questions reached the ears of Sweden's parliamentarians. Now, all she had to do was wait for their responses.

But the strike in Stockholm was only the beginning.

2

reta was not always a brave hero, famous all over the world for her determination. Before starting her mission in front of the Swedish Parliament, she was a wary, quiet, shy girl. The kind of student who doesn't speak in class and sits to one side, somewhere up the back. Nothing particularly exciting had happened in her life, or at least nothing that would make you think that one day she would convince hundreds of thousands of children to follow her example.

But environmental issues had always

interested her. She was just a little girl when she first heard people talking about them. At eight years of age, she found out that the planet's climate was changing irreversibly.

At school, her teachers often reminded the children that in order to save electricity it was important to turn off the lights every time they left a room, and that they shouldn't waste water or food. All these suggestions made Greta curious, and she asked them a simple question: "Why?"

They explained that people were changing the climate with their behaviour.

To Greta, this immediately sounded quite serious. If it was true, then we should all be really worried. You didn't have to be a rocket scientist to understand that this was a big problem. Even to her, as a little girl, it sounded horrifying. And yet, unbelievably, the grown-ups didn't seem too worried. This was the biggest worry of all!

How was it possible that none of the grown-ups she knew were doing anything to fix the problem that was staring them in the face.

Why were other, less important issues being discussed on television, in the papers and on the internet, and not this one?

How could everyone go on calmly about their business while the world was being threatened with an environmental catastrophe?

Greta couldn't find an answer to these questions. She ended up feeling very, very sad. The adults might not have been worried, but she was.

There was something else about Greta that set her apart from her schoolmates, other than her strong interest in the environment.

At the age of 11, the doctors had diagnosed her with Asperger's syndrome.

People who suffer from Asperger's often become interested in a particular issue and think about it obsessively without being able to let go. This is exactly what was happening to Greta.

Most of us are overwhelmed every day by lots of different stories, information and news. They have an impact on us, they affect our feelings, they worry us, but pretty soon – almost always – we forget about them, because we are so caught up in the things we're doing. We might be really worried about pollution, but then we end up moving those thoughts to a tiny corner of our minds, we hop in the car or on a scooter to drive over to visit our best friend, without thinking about exhaust fumes and how they poison the air. For Greta, it wasn't so easy. Her brain works in a slightly different way to most people's. For her, the world is black or white, there are situations that are right and others that are wrong. You can't just decide that pollution is terrible and then keep on polluting the planet in your everyday life.

At school one day when Greta was still little, the teacher showed the class a documentary on plastic pollution in the ocean.

The film showed starving polar bears and other animals in distress. Like all the other children in the class, Greta was very moved and worried by the story. She cried all the way through the film. However, when the lights were turned on at the end, her classmates started thinking about other things: recess, what to do after school, tomorrow's homework. But Greta found she couldn't do that. The images of the planet polluted by plastic were stuck in her head and refused to go away.

Because she was so interested in the environment, Greta had once entered a competition run by a Swedish daily newspaper, the *Svenska Dagbladet*. She did some research and wrote an article. Her entry was judged to be the best and she won the competition. The article was published and several activists (people committed to protecting the environment) contacted the young writer, curious about such a well-informed schoolgirl.

Thanks to the newspaper, Greta was able to get to know people who shared her concerns. They were trying to draw the rest of the country's attention to the issue, by starting discussions and searching for solutions. Unfortunately, none of their many ideas convinced enough people, and nothing happened. But Greta was not ready to give up.

Greta's mind worked in another very special way: she would focus intently on something that interested her. Asperger's syndrome makes people determined and capable of extraordinary commitment. For years, Greta did in-depth research into climate change, building up a wealth of information, which was unusual for a girl her age.

She knew as much about it as an adult expert might. During a school outing to a museum, she noticed that some of the information about carbon dioxide written on the wall panels was wrong. She became very angry about the error – so much so that she left the class group, dropped out of the tour and went and sat by herself near the entrance to the museum.

The more she read, the more her discoveries worried her. She wondered what her future would be like if the temperature of the planet continued to increase. Her thoughts were dark and terrifying, and difficult to face without being overcome by depression.

Unfortunately, Greta had never been a talkative girl, so she kept her turmoil to herself until she became so sad and depressed that she could no longer leave the house in the morning to go to school.

Then, at the age of 11, the sadness became an

illness. It was as if something inside her had suddenly cracked. The doctors called it depression.

She stopped talking and reading and even eating. In two months, she lost approximately ten kilograms. She didn't feel life was worth living, because there was too much injustice in the world. She couldn't explain what was happening to her and she was silent and despairing.

Her parents, Svante Thunberg and Malena Ernman, wondered if something had happened at school, but her teachers said no. They said that Greta was too quiet, that she tended to cut herself off from the others and hardly spoke.

Her mother struggled to understand – to her, that didn't seem to be such a big problem. She had been quiet and introverted as a young girl herself.

What was the big deal? As Malena grew up,

she had found comfort in her music. Singing had helped her become more confident and find her place in the world.

This was a very difficult time for Malena Ernman, as she tried to meet her work commitments and deal with her daughter's illness.

She was the star of a major show in Stockholm, singing and dancing in front of thousands of spectators. It should have been a happy time, but performing in front of an audience when you know that your daughters are unwell at home is terrible.

You see, while Greta was struggling with depression, her sister, Beata, also started showing signs of illness. She could not handle confusion, noise bothered her, and she found it difficult to attend classes, just like Greta.

The two sisters were seen by lots of doctors, who tried to understand exactly what was going on for them. It wasn't easy, but finally they were able to give a name to what made Greta and Beata different: Asperger's syndrome.

At that point Greta's parents started looking for a solution that would allow the two girls to return to a normal life, one step at a time.

For people with Asperger's, situations that are absolutely normal to other people can be very challenging for them. Daily life can be very complicated, and Greta and Beata could not go back to their previous routine.

Greta's parents were very committed to supporting their daughters. It was a serious situation: they stopped working to help them get through this difficult time.

Greta was unable to attend classes with her schoolfriends and no-one could convince her, so she didn't go to school for a year. She sat quietly on the couch at home. However, her parents' first concern was convincing her to start eating again.

Apart from going to doctors' appointments, there wasn't much for her to do to pass the time. The days dragged by in the Thunbergs' large timber house at the top of a hill, and her sadness refused to lift. Things changed the day Greta managed to open up.

She realised that by talking about her fears with her mum and dad she felt a bit better. Her parents were very alert to what was going on in the world around them. They believed that everyone had the right to live in peace.

Greta pointed out that they were right to be concerned about the human race, but they were forgetting one essential aspect: the environment people lived in. While they were worried about people fleeing wars, they continued to travel, eat meat and drive big cars, and were therefore damaging the planet.

In the beginning, Svante and Malena tried to reassure their daughter that everything would turn out for the best. However, while she liked sharing her ideas and being listened to, Greta knew perfectly well that problems don't just solve themselves, especially big ones like climate change.

Because she wasn't going to school, Greta had more time on her hands than before. She decided it would be a good idea to explain her point of view more clearly. Her mother and father listened to her and were happy to discuss environmental issues with her, but they had never really understood how serious the situation was. So Greta started showing them photos, statistics, graphs and other information.

She sat down with them on the sofa and showed them movies and documentaries. She gave them newspaper articles and reports written by respected journalists.

After being faced with this information, Greta's parents were no longer only concerned about their daughter. The planet wasn't doing too well either.

Might it be possible that Greta was right and that everyone else was making a big mistake by not taking the environment seriously enough?

Svante and Malena realised that they and their unsustainable lifestyle were the problem.

This came as a big shock to them.

Greta could not accept that her family lived so irresponsibly. Suddenly, thanks to her, they opened their eyes to the importance of the environment.

Something had changed: they had started to really listen to what their daughter was saying. They no longer just talked to her to make her feel better. They were now really interested, worried and alert to the issues that were close to her heart.

This was what changed things. Greta, who in the meantime had turned fifteen, understood that it might make all the difference. Just as she had convinced her mother and father, she might be able to change the minds of other people. There was a lot to do and gradually she overcame her depression with a new sense of purpose.

Malena, a famous opera singer, and Svante, an actor and writer who was very well-known in Sweden, changed their opinions thanks to their daughter. Their work often took them around the world. Malena, in particular, went on concert tours.

Greta had made her think about the environmental impact of every aeroplane she boarded to travel to a city far away, perhaps on the other side of the world. In order to lift hundreds of passengers and their baggage into the sky, aircraft engines burn large quantities of fuel and release carbon dioxide, which builds up in the atmosphere and raises the temperature of the planet.

One day Malena went to Tokyo for an important concert, which was broadcast on television and watched by a large audience. It was an exciting occasion, because it meant she was reaching out to a totally new audience.

When she got home, Greta talked to her about the environmental impact of the trip she had just been on. It didn't make sense to be happy about success in her work and just ignore the negative impact on the environment.

Many aspects of the Thunbergs' lifestyle could be criticised, not only their air travel. Greta patiently explained it all to her parents. Because she'd done her research, she was well-prepared. She quoted scientists and answered her mum and dad's questions.

Svante and Malena knew very little about these issues. They had just a vague idea. In the beginning they tried to fight back, but soon they ran out of excuses. Greta was always right.

She set an example, deciding she would be very careful about the things she bought. If something wasn't absolutely necessary, she would do without. She decided she would no longer travel by air. If she couldn't go on holidays to exotic, faraway places, that was just too bad. In Stockholm, she rode her bike and wasn't at all concerned about the cold, which in Sweden can be particularly severe. The cold, the rain and the snow are only a problem if you don't dress properly. For longer journeys, she caught the train.

Not only did her parents accept these decisions, they ended up following her example. On her frequent work-related trips, Malena

Thunberg no longer travelled by air.

For years, Malena had moved from one part of the world to the other, taking her family with her.

When Greta was a baby, the Thunberg family travelled from one theatre to another.

Of course, they couldn't leave baby Greta at home by herself, so for a while Svante stopped working as an actor in order to accompany his wife on tour and look after their daughters. He decided to sacrifice his career to look after his family.

Beata was born soon after Greta. With two babies, there was no option: at least one of the two parents had to take time off work. Svante didn't like the idea of giving up the stage to raise his baby girls. Besides, he enjoyed travelling.

When Greta and Beata were older, the Thunbergs settled in Stockholm, but Malena continued with her busy concert schedule, even travelling abroad to places that could only be reached by plane.

After Greta convinced her, she gave up her international career. She preferred being a little less famous and playing her part in protecting the environment. Mr Thunberg became a vegetarian like his daughter. Thanks to the books Greta showed them, he discovered how much intensive animal farming pollutes the environment. They started growing vegetables in a small garden just outside the city, installed solar panels and bought an electric car to be used only when absolutely necessary. For everyday travel, they rode their regular bikes.

A little at a time, the Thunbergs got rid of all the bad habits and behaviours that were harmful to the planet.

Greta had won her first battle!

Greta had always paid attention to climate change, but the summer of 2018 was a turning point. The weather was incredibly hot, much more so than normal.

Swedish people wore singlets and tried to keep cool by dipping their feet in the cold waters of the Baltic Sea. Many people would say there's nothing strange about that. After all, it was summer, right?

But Sweden is in Scandinavia, which is tucked away in the northern part of the world's maps.

A Scandinavian summer is like springtime in the European countries near the Mediterranean. The air is a bit warm and the sun shines, but it isn't as hot as in southern Europe.

However, in 2018, the temperature reached record highs. The highest ever recorded in 262 years.

While warm temperatures can be nice for people who aren't familiar with global warming, fires are a real problem that everybody understands. Wildfires can be catastrophic. And that summer there were lots of wildfires in Scandinavia.

Fires were burning everywhere, even in the remote north. In the region called Lapland, something occurred that had never happened before: more than sixty fires devastated entire forests. This was partly due to the high temperatures, the dry climate, and the fact that it hadn't rained in almost two months.

The small number of firefighters working in the north fought the blazes non-stop, and they called for help and reinforcements to deal with the situation.

They were unprepared for the fires. Volunteers, helicopters and even the army were called in, but the blazes seemed unstoppable.

Entire villages were evacuated because it was too dangerous to remain close to the fires. Black smoke turned the sky dark.

Firefighters and ordinary people, such as Gunnar Lundstom, the chief firefighter in the village of Jokkmokk, battled the fires for almost two consecutive days without rest.

The temperature rose to 30°C, an unbelievable temperature for freezing Lapland, which spends most of the year under a blanket of snow.

Everyone talked about what was going on. Newspapers with dramatic headlines arrived in the shops, but no-one did anything practical.

No-one except Greta.

Actually, compared to many other countries around the world, Sweden takes its environmental problems quite seriously.

Swedish politicians are aware of how bad the situation is and have tried to tackle it. They were the first country in the Western world to draft and pass a law to reduce greenhouse gas emissions, with an ambitious goal of reducing them to zero by the year 2045. If everyone behaved like the Swedes, we would certainly be doing the planet a big favour.

However, for Greta, this wasn't enough. More was needed, and it needed to be done without waiting all those years. This is what the scientists said and there was no reason why she shouldn't believe them.

Furthermore, the issue had been practically ignored recently. This was a concern, because in the months leading up to the election politicians from the various parties discussed their views on the issues they considered most important in the newspapers, on television and on the internet. They explained what they would do if they were elected and tried to convince voters to vote for them and their ideas. If there was an important issue, it was addressed and discussed during the election campaign.

But despite the fires that had devastated the country during the summer, there was very little political discussion about climate change. Politicians did not seem particularly interested in the issue.

It would take someone with courage to draw their attention to it and remind them what the real priorities should be.

This is why the weeks leading up to the election were so important for Greta.

3

reta's protest attracted a lot of attention. Swedish politicians and the ordinary people who would soon be voting became more aware of environmental issues, and remembered the commitment made a few years earlier by governments all over the world, a commitment many seemed to have forgotten.

The United Nations Climate Change Conference took place in France, just three years earlier. In 2015, politicians from 195 countries – practically all the countries of the world! – met in Paris to discuss climate change.

For some time, scientists had been aware of a very worrying phenomenon: the temperature of the planet was steadily rising.

The scientists who monitor global warming had noticed to their dismay that over the past century temperatures had been increasing. Winters were less harsh and summers were hotter. They worked hard on the problem until they found an explanation: it was all because of greenhouse gases produced by the earth's human population. These gases end up high above us, gathered in the sky. They let the sun's rays through, but they capture the heat and never let it go. Of all the greenhouse gases, the one with the biggest concentration in the sky is carbon dioxide, which humanity produces in large quantities.

This is why representatives of 195 countries went to Paris. Their aim was to develop an agreement to produce and release less carbon dioxide into the environment and therefore limit global warming as much as possible.

A one-degree rise in temperature doesn't sound like much: you would expect it to be barely noticeable. Yet, the damage it can do is enormous. As temperatures rise, the ice caps melt. The ice around the North and South Poles shrinks, and snowfalls on the tops of mountains decrease. All that melted ice ends up in the ocean and the sea level rises.

As a result, the climate changes: it rains when it shouldn't, some places become deserts and the rivers dry up.

The consequences are catastrophic.

Greta knew this all too well and decided to take action. She was convinced that a school strike organised by children was a great idea.

She was inspired by a group of brave American children who started a protest on the other side of the ocean by not going to school.

A few months before Greta started campaigning with her placard outside the Swedish Parliament, a group of American students had gone on a school strike to let everybody know how angry and worried they were about the laws that allowed people to buy firearms very easily. Handguns and rifles of all kinds were available to anyone and easily ended up in the hands of criminals, with tragic consequences.

Recently, at the Marjory Stoneman Douglas school in Florida, a boy had walked through the corridors and started shooting. American students no longer felt safe in the classrooms where they studied every day, and they wanted the politicians who ran the country to know this.

Greta heard about this and was curious.

Refusing to walk into your classroom, deciding instead to go out into the streets and tell everyone what you think really sounded like a smart idea.

It isn't always easy for children to make the adults they know listen to them. Imagine trying to get politicians to pay attention!

If news about the gun control protests had made it as far as Sweden, clearly the young American students had found a way to spread the word.

4

Greta's parents understood what she was trying to do, but they didn't agree that she should skip school. They told her quite clearly that their job was to make sure she attended classes. They asked her if there really was no other way for her to make her voice heard, but she said no, there wasn't.

At age fifteen you can't even vote, so there was no other way she could make her case.

Although Malena and Svante shared their daughter's concerns, school was the priority. However, they remembered that when Greta was miserable she wouldn't even leave the house, so they had to admit that protesting outside the parliament in support of her beliefs had made her feel better. She seemed to have rediscovered a little spark that she had lost during her depression.

A lot of her teachers also felt it was wrong not to attend classes, and they let her know. Greta ignored them all, convinced that she was right. Perhaps by skipping school she would end up in trouble, but she was prepared to suffer the consequences of her choices.

"I'm doing it because no-one else cares," she said.

The evidence said she was right.

Or at least it showed that a lot of people agreed with her.

On the 7th of September, election day and the day of Greta's biggest climate strike yet, a large crowd of people sat on the ground in front of the parliament building.

Greta's determination had woken people up and something was changing. The Swedes and many other people around the world

SCHOOL STRIKE FOR THE CLIMATE

were turning their attention to the wellbeing of the planet and to the girl with plaits holding a placard.

Happy with what had been achieved so far, Greta was now ready for new challenges and situations that previously she would have found difficult to deal with.

The day after the election, she prepared a speech for the People's Climate March, a big rally held on the same day in several cities around the world. Thousands of people marched, demanding that those in power organise serious initiatives to stop the climate disaster. Even in Stockholm there was a march through the city which then gathered in Mynttorget Square, where several climate change activists spoke from a podium. The organisers had also asked Greta to speak. This was precisely the kind of situation that could be a problem for her.

Her parents were worried. People with Asperger's syndrome can often become very afraid, more than other people; they are overwhelmed by uncontrollable anxiety, which prevents them from speaking, simply blocking their speech. This happens particularly when they are addressing a person they have never met before or – even worse! – a group of people. It's not simple shyness, which can happen to anybody. Speaking becomes really impossible and you cannot be persuaded to open your mouth no matter how gently you are asked to. Doctors have given this a fancy name: selective mutism.

Svante and Malena tried to warn their daughter. Did she really feel like doing this? Was she ready to tackle a situation like that? But Greta, like all teenagers, and maybe even more than most of them, could be stubborn once she had made a decision. She was not prepared to compromise on the issues she cared about. She would go ahead and address the rally.

Under a grey sky, Greta gripped the microphone, held on tightly to the sheet on which she had written her notes, and spoke to the dozens of people in the crowd. When she got to the end, the audience applauded. They were moved by the words of the teenager with the plaits.

On the same day as the People's Climate March, Greta announced her decision: she would continue with the school strike, sitting outside the Parliament building every Friday. She planned to continue until Sweden achieved all the goals that its political representatives had announced at the Paris conference.

They had promised, after all.

Global warming had to be reduced and the increase in temperature kept below 2°C, with the aim of not going over 1.5°C. The politicians had signed the Paris Agreement, so why not commit to taking action on it immediately?

On her Instagram profile, Greta invited everyone to take part and join her every Friday in front of the Riksdag. Her invitation was very clear.

There is a lot less time than we think, she said. Failure will bring disaster.

Having decided on her strategy, the following Monday Greta went back to school, to the great relief of her parents and teachers.

But her struggle continued.

Greta was encouraged by the crowd that

had gathered on election day for the *skolstrejk för klimatet* and the interest people had shown in the climate march. She was now confident that out there, and not just in Stockholm, there were a lot of people prepared to support her fight.

They needed to become involved and had to be convinced to take action.

She recorded a message in a short video, which she then posted on Instagram, explaining in English the reasons behind her strike. She wanted to be sure that everybody understood what she was saying, even outside Sweden.

Her fellow citizens soon showed how interested they were: by the last Friday of September, rallies were already being held in Malmö, Gothenburg and many other Swedish cities. They were all demanding immediate, decisive action to stop global warming.

Journalists also supported Greta. They were more and more interested in the story of the 15-year-old who skipped classes as a form of protest.

They all wanted to interview her. They came from all over the world and had a lot of questions for her: How did she get the idea to strike? What did her parents and teachers think? What motivates a 15-year-old to become so interested in the environment?

Greta answered their questions, although she didn't really feel like talking about herself. The welfare of the planet seemed like a much more interesting and important topic. But she accepted an invitation to take part in a television broadcast and held meetings in several Swedish cities.

It was tiring having to deal with so many strangers, but Greta had a deep understanding of the issue and could speak clearly about the problem of climate change.

Over the years, she had become a real expert.

When the famous American magazine *The New Yorker* interviewed her and the reporter wrote in the article that greenhouse gas emissions had gone down, Greta did not hesitate to point out that what had been said in the article was wrong. It didn't matter that the article had been written by the reporter of a famous magazine; you have to be honest and tell the truth.

All kinds of different statistics can be used to illustrate a complex problem like global warming. Politicians often choose the most favourable ones, highlighting the progress that has been made to avoid revealing how serious the situation still is.

But it is only fair that people know the truth. It is childish to kid yourself that there isn't a problem.

Ironically, it took a 15-year-old to point this out to the country's politicians.

5

reta's hard work was yielding results and was reaching far beyond the footpath in front of the Swedish Riksdag. She caught a train to the European Parliament in Brussels, Belgium, to take part in a rally and continue her battle for the environment. In Brussels, she gave a presentation in French, talking about her school strike and pointing out that in Sweden people lived as if they had the resources of 4.2 planets at their disposal, which is obviously ridiculous.

She then went on to Helsinki in Finland to

address a packed city square, reminding her audience about the millions of barrels of oil we use every day so that we can maintain our current lifestyle.

Then she was off to London.

To travel around Europe, she needed her parents' support and permission.

Greta's parents decided they would help her and encourage her to pursue her campaign. They were on her side. And they were also prepared to travel according to their daughter's rules.

Travelling internationally by land was slow and difficult. There were trains to catch, connections to make and lots of waiting in stations.

But the alternative was long journeys in the family's electric car, which needed to be recharged frequently.

Greta wasn't afraid of hard work. In fact,

where the environment was concerned, there wasn't much that could hold her back.

Generally speaking, she had always been a girl who obeyed the rules, but by now she had reached the conclusion that she could not solve the problem without rebelling. The laws were not achieving what they were supposed to, and the planet was in danger.

This was exactly the thinking of the protesters who, like Greta, gathered in London at the end of October outside the British Parliament.

"There is a tremendous emergency that no-one treats as a crisis, while the leaders in our countries are behaving immaturely. We need to wake up and change things," said Greta, addressing the crowd.

On their banners, the Rebels – as many of those who gathered that day in London's Parliament Square called themselves – pointed out that humanity was facing one of its darkest hours. The science was clearly saying that we face catastrophe if we don't act quickly.

As she travelled around Europe in the weeks after the Swedish elections, Greta discovered that around the world there were many other people engaged in struggles like hers. This was not the only discovery she made. She also realised that she wasn't at all nervous when speaking in public about the issues she was familiar with.

She wasn't the kind of girl who enjoyed or was good at small talk, but she was very good at making serious speeches with a microphone in her hand.

Svante and Malena were proud to hear their daughter speak in front of hundreds, even thousands, of strangers, often in English.

It was also a bit surprising. In just a few months, they saw Greta change from being a quiet, sad girl to being a respected champion of environmental activism.

Greta's courage and ideas spread quickly all over the world. Even in faraway Australia, which was literally on the other side of the world, many children decided to skip school as a form of protest.

While this was astonishing, what happened afterwards was even more incredible: the Australian prime minister – the most powerful politician in the country, himself! – officially asked the children to go back to school. On Instagram, Greta replied: "I am sorry, Prime Minister Scott Morrison, but we cannot obey."

Greta's slowly growing fame was incredible.

In just a few weeks, the most popular and famous newspapers were talking about her, and a few months after the first school strike, she was invited to speak at TED.

TED stands for "Technology, Entertainment, Design", and it is an organisation that hosts talks on important issues. Experts in various fields walk onto a stage and give lectures on subjects they understand deeply.

In recent decades, some of the most famous people in the world have stood on the TED stage and addressed audiences of millions of people.

It was a prestigious and important invitation.

Greta talked about justice. Wouldn't it be fair if the countries with the most developed economies reduced their impact on the environment to allow other countries to continue building roads, hospitals and everything else that people need to lead better lives?

She also noted that no politician has ever made a commitment to seeking a long-term solution. The bravest politicians talked about taking action on goals to be achieved by 2050, which seems very far into the future, but isn't really.

By 2050, the children of today will be adults and will still have many years ahead of them. What will become of them after that if we don't stop climate change?

What do today's adults intend to do for the future of their children?

Every TED talk usually ends with a message of hope. This was not the case with Greta's presentation.

"Much more than hope, we need action," she said.

6

The world's leaders were behaving childishly. They ignored environmental problems because they were afraid of how complex they were.

So the children, who were worried about their own futures, decided to protest to convince the politicians. And the school strike that Greta Thunberg had started, all by herself, outside the Swedish Parliament in August 2018 was only the first step.

In just a few months, the number of cities where people, many of them schoolchildren, were protesting had reached 270. More than 20,000 students in every corner of the world had stopped going to school, following the example of the *skolstrejk för klimatet*.

Having encouraged so many children to take action, Greta was then ready to tackle a new goal. To convince world leaders to take real action, not just talk about the problem.

To achieve this, in December 2018 she went to Katowice, a small city in Poland, to take part in a gathering with an unusual name: COP24. She went there in an electric car and it took two days, but it was worth it.

COP24 is an event where representatives from almost every country meet to discuss climate change. It is organised by the United Nations, a global organisation established to help politicians agree on important issues.

The people responsible for preventing an environmental catastrophe arrived in Katowice in serious-looking black motorcars. Would they be able to make the right decisions and action them straightaway?

Many people doubted it.

Greta packed her case and set off. She was due to meet a man with a very important job: the Secretary of the United Nations, Antonio Guterres. He was usually dealing with big natural disasters and trying to stop wars.

Greta found herself in a white-walled hall with a large rectangular table, which was also white. The hall felt official and cold. The leaders of various countries were seated around the table. In front of each of them was a microphone and a card with their name written on it.

In front of the large audience seated in the stalls, Greta climbed onto the stage. She was wearing the same checked shirt that she wore on the first day of her *skolstrejk för klimatet*. For Greta, formal clothes were definitely not a priority given the really urgent matters that had to be discussed. Behind her, an enormous banner, with the unmistakable blue flag of the United Nations, made it clear where she was. A serious-sounding voice introduced her.

In front of the delegates, Greta was not intimidated.

"Over the past 25 years, countless people have come to United Nations climate conferences imploring our leaders to stop emissions, and this obviously hasn't worked. So I will not implore you to protect our future. We have been ignored in the past and we will be ignored in future. I'm here to tell you that things are going to change, whether you like it or not," she said.

On that stage, Greta stressed the urgent need to face up to reality, no matter how disturbing, and encouraged people to imagine what was possible if everyone made an effort.

If children can end up on the front pages of newspapers for a school strike, then there is nothing that cannot be achieved. Despite the fact that there were powerful people who usually issued orders listening to her in the audience, she found the courage to accuse them all of behaving like little children, frightened at the thought of being unpopular.

She reminded them about the damage already done to the environment, explaining that it would be future generations who would take responsibility for change, if no-one else was prepared to do it. She urged the audience to reflect on the fate of their children, who were being condemned to live in a world that was more and more devastated. You cannot fix a crisis if you don't treat it like one.

This had never happened before. Never had a teenage girl reminded the world's most powerful about their mistakes, telling them off and encouraging them to change. Many applauded her, despite the harsh criticism she gave.

United Nations meetings are long and tedious. Delegates spend entire days discussing problems and negotiating solutions.

Everything is written down in official documents, but all that hard work often produces only small changes in people's lives.

This is what happened in Poland under Greta's own eyes. She felt that no real decisions were made.

During the second week of meetings, she switched on her mobile phone and recorded a video.

In a room at the conference centre where the COP24 was being held, she introduced herself and explained that, once again, politicians were not coming up with any solutions, despite the fact that scientists were more certain than ever of how serious the situation was.

> WHOEVER YOU ARE,
> WHEREVER YOU MIGHT BE,
> WE NEED YOU!
> JOIN THE GENERAL CLIMATE
> STRIKE THIS FRIDAY.
> PLEASE, STRIKE WITH US!
> SHARE THE VIDEO, LET THE
> WORLD KNOW.

Meanwhile, outside, a crowd of protesters had gathered in the streets of Katowice. They wanted to be heard and to show the politicians who had travelled to Poland for COP24 that a lot of people were really worried about the environment.

The openness and honesty with which the young Swedish girl spoke to world leaders was amazing.

Just as incredible was the way in which she convinced people to take action.

Time, the prestigious and iconic American weekly magazine, named Greta one of the most influential teens of 2018.

This was a great honour, which she had absolutely earned.

However, Greta was not the type to congratulate herself for her achievements. So at the end of the United Nations COP24 meeting, she immediately left Poland and returned home, in the family's electric car. She had an appointment she could not miss: the climate strike in Malmö.

Greta had no intention of stopping, not before she had achieved her goal: saving the planet.

7

There are a lot of people in the world who have made protecting the environment their life's work and have dedicated themselves to it wholeheartedly. However, Greta could not do this, because at the age of 15 she had obligations and commitments she could not ignore.

Just like the most committed activists, Greta travelled around Europe organising strikes to protect the environment, writing speeches and preparing presentations. In order to speak in front of thousands of people, sometimes in a foreign language, you need to do your homework and get on top of general information and a lot of detail.

Not only did the cause she was fighting for require commitment, but she herself had now become a celebrity. Journalists from every nation asked if she was available for interviews and famous reporters wanted to know everything about her and her ideas. Although she didn't particularly like talking about herself, Greta agreed to do so because it meant putting the environment on the front pages of newspapers and raising the profile of her cause.

On top of this were commitments that professional activists did not have: the commitments of any 15-year-old girl. There was homework to do and lessons to catch up on so that she didn't fall behind her classmates. Greta had started going to school again and skipped classes for the *skolstrejk för klimatet* only on

Fridays. She still ventured into the city centre on weekends to protest. She did so in rain and snow, even on the coldest and darkest days of the Swedish winter.

She really had a lot of commitments taking up her time from early morning until late at night. She didn't have much time to spend with her sister Beata, the rest of her family or her two dogs. She almost didn't have enough time to sleep: at six in the morning she would get up ready to face a new day. Whenever she felt tired, she remembered what had led her to becoming the famous girl in plaits, took a deep breath and got on with it.

Reassured by her good marks at school and her decision to return to classes, Greta's parents decided to help their daughter.

Greta really needed her parents' support: at 15, she couldn't go travelling around the world by herself. Svante went with her, travelling across Europe on long train journeys or driving the electric car. With his open smile and his long brown hair gathered in a plait, Svante was the perfect ally for Greta. He knew how to talk to people and felt comfortable alongside her even on the podiums of the biggest conferences in the world. He was ready to help his daughter with the ambitious goal she had set herself: saving the planet. Journalists would sometimes interview him as well, and there wasn't a question he couldn't answer.

Greta needed her father's help, because she had more and more commitments and they were becoming increasingly demanding. She was invited to Panama, New York, San Francisco and Canada. She couldn't accept these invitations because it would have meant flying. But she could commit to visiting places that were closer. Some invitations were very, very important. She was asked to attend the Davos forum at the end of January 2019. Davos is a quiet town in Switzerland. Graceful buildings and wooden houses are scattered along a valley between tall mountains, lush forests and ski runs. Every year since the 1970s, in late January, leading politicians, celebrated economic experts, intellectuals, journalists and scientists meet to discuss the most urgent issues that the world needs to confront.

The World Economic Forum is a unique event. The powerful meet in this small mountain town that for the rest of the year is a quiet ski resort in the Alps. They take part in meetings and conferences, get to know each other and work together to develop solutions. Only the participants know what is said at Davos, because meetings are held behind closed doors. This secrecy, together with the status of the participants, makes the Davos forum a highly exclusive event. To take part, you must be invited. And only the people who really count are on the list. One of these was Greta.

Greta set off on her journey on a cold January morning, wearing a scarf, a hat and a heavy coat and carrying a red suitcase and her ever-present *skolstrejk för klimatet* placard. She was at the station ready to travel south before the sun came up. She crossed Scania, the southern region of Sweden, and then Denmark. Finally, having arrived in Germany, she boarded a night train to Zurich, Switzerland.

After travelling more than thirty hours to get to Davos, Greta was met at the station by a group of reporters with television cameras and microphones. On the platform, holding her placard, she answered their questions, saying that one day she wanted to be able to look back and know that she had done the right thing. She didn't check into one of the many hotels but instead moved into Arctic Base Camp, a large tent like the ones used by Arctic explorers, pitched right next to the famous Schatzalp Hotel. This unique accommodation was the idea of an organisation that wanted to remind people about the consequences that the rising temperatures had on the perennial ice of the North and South Poles.

Despite the freezing cold of the Swiss winter, when temperatures at night drop many degrees below zero, Greta fell asleep in her yellow sleeping bag.

The next day, she spoke at a meeting and reminded people that we are all responsible for climate change.

Famous singers will.i.am and Bono, as well as diplomats and scientists, heard Greta speak. Jane Goodall, the brave English scientist who had lived with chimpanzees and shown everyone how much like people they are, was there too. Greta took a photo with her as a souvenir.

Greta was not intimidated by the well-known faces in the audience, by how famous the people in front of her were, or by the impressive names and positions. As always, she repeated her message. It made no difference whether she was speaking to a small group of students or to the world's leaders.

Dressed like any other ordinary girl her age, surrounded by men with serious faces wearing dark suits, she climbed up to the podium and spoke.

"Adults keep saying that they must give young people hope. I don't want hope, I want you to panic, to take action. I want you to behave as if you were in the middle of a crisis, because that's what it is."

"Our house is on fire: our house, planet earth, is going up in flames. And the adults, the powerful, must act responsibly and act for the future of young people."

She then took part in the climate strike in the streets of Davos, together with other young people her age who were just as worried about the situation.

The next day, she was already on the way back, tackling the long journey to Sweden, catching one train after another, heading north.

The harsh words a 15-year-old girl had directed at the world's leaders caught many people's attention. Greta succeeded in doing something that seemed impossible: drawing the world's attention to the climate crisis. She reminded the French president, the leaders of the European Union and all the politicians at Davos about the need to take urgent action.

When journalists asked her if she was optimistic about seeing the world take an interest in the issue, she said she wasn't. The only thing that really mattered were the greenhouse gas emissions in the atmosphere, which were still not going down.

That famous people who were listening to her speak and nodding their heads did not matter if decisions were not followed by action.

8

Only eight months from the day Greta decided to skip school in order to strike, a lot had changed. One of the changes was particularly important: the world, finally, had started to understand the seriousness of the situation.

There were more and more strikes and protests outside parliament buildings and in streets all over the world. It was mostly children and teens who were marching, determined to force the "grown-ups" to accept responsibility.

The movement, made up of thousands of young people who mobilised every Friday, now had a name: Fridays for Future. The common goal of all the young protesters was to remind the politicians of the importance of taking immediate action.

There was one politician in particular who could make all the difference. He was the head of the European Commission in Brussels.

That's where Greta went in February 2019.

Brussels was Greta's next target, for a series of events that had been initiated a long time ago, when no-one was talking about global warming yet.

In 1957, people living in Europe still had vivid memories of the Second World War and all the suffering and horrors it brought.

The leaders of six nations – France, West Germany, Italy, Belgium, the Netherlands and

Luxembourg – decided to form an 'economic community', which meant from then on they would cooperate to make sure their economies grew together rather than against each other. The Europe we know today, where people can travel and move around freely, without borders to stop them, evolved from that first meeting. Europeans quickly realised that everything worked a lot better when you joined forces, and other countries decided to follow the example of the first six. Nowadays, many important decisions are not made in Europe's parliaments, but by the representatives of each country in the institutions of the European Union.

Just outside Brussels, there is an entire district where the headquarters of European organisations are situated. They are large buildings with glass windows. Their design is modern and austere, with lots of flapping flags. That's where Greta was headed.

Speaking seriously and critically, she said that you can't just hope that problems will fix themselves. If the men and women in power had done their research, they would know how serious the situation was and how important it was to take urgent action.

In the large room where they had gathered, European politicians listened in silence while the world's media pointed television cameras at Greta.

"We are fixing the chaos that you created and we will not stop until we have finished," she announced in a firm voice.

And it had to be done now. There was no time left to wait for the next generation to grow up and take their turn as leaders.

Some important politicians, like the United Kingdom's prime minister, Theresa May, had recently criticised students for marching in the streets instead of going to school. Greta used this opportunity in Brussels to respond to them.

"I would like to remind people who say that we are wasting precious time by not going to school, that our politicians have wasted decades in denying there was a problem and doing nothing to fix it."

She then suggested to those same people who were worried about missed school days to go on strike in the students' place, and skip work. Or even better, they could join the young people and protest together in order to achieve the desired result more quickly, so the children could then go back to their schoolwork.

On the 15th of March 2019, it wasn't only Greta's voice that made itself heard. Thousands of people all over the world protested during the great worldwide strike for the future. While in August the year before only Greta had sat in front of the Riksdag, there were now 123 countries and more than two thousand cities involved. In Italy alone, one million young people took part.

On that not-so-distant late summer day it would have been very hard to imagine that just a few months later thousands of people would gather in Stockholm at the invitation of a 15-year-old girl with plaits and a lot of courage.

Some people came from very far away to protest, including the United States.

Many of them wanted to have their photos taken with Greta. They wanted to shake her hand and thank her.

When she climbed onto the stage, the crowd gave her a rousing round of applause.

Some people were reminded of Rosa Parks,

the African-American woman who in 1955 refused to stand up and give her seat to a "white" man on a bus in Montgomery, Alabama. With one simple gesture, Rosa sparked a series of protests and rallies that led to a historic decision by the Supreme Court: the most important judges in America decided that to separate people in that way, by the colour of their skin, was wrong.

By refusing to give up her seat, Rosa Parks wasn't saying anything new – nothing that Alabama's African-Americans didn't already know. But she succeeded in inspiring them and convinced them to take action until things changed. Rosa Parks was one of the women who had always fascinated and inspired Greta.

An enormous number of children and teenagers protested on the 15th of March 2019.

They were the heart and soul of the rallies, worried about the problems created by generations of people who came before them.

Reporters interviewed them, asking complicated questions about what the solutions might be. Someone even referred to the occasion as "the revolt of the young".

On the podium, a girl said that students were protesting and demanding solutions, but they didn't have a magic wand that could stop global warming. People had to listen to the scientists, they would have to examine the situation and become better informed. There were no easy fixes to prevent temperatures from rising.

Greta and all those protesting with her will not stop until the grown-ups, the politicians and the powerful *do* something.

They are the ones responsible for finding out what needs to be done and then actually doing it.

9

reta does not have easy answers for fixing the problem. Her aim is to draw the attention of the world's leaders to the climate changes that scientists are talking about. She often says, "It is not the children who can decide what to do."

Not taking action is so dangerous: changes to the climate are making life on earth more and more difficult. Environmental disasters risk causing wars and conflicts. The commitment of young people to Fridays for Future is therefore a commitment to peace.

Thanks to her incredible achievements, Greta was nominated for the 2019 Nobel Peace Prize. She would not be the first young woman to be nominated, or to win. In 2014, 17-year-old Malala Yousafzai won it for the courage she showed in fighting for the rights of children and youth in her country, Pakistan, where the cruel Taliban had banned girls from going to school.

"It is a great inspiration to see young people, led by young women, speaking out," said the mayor of Paris, Anne Hidalgo.

To her critics, Greta responds by saying they should become better informed, listen to the scientists and scholars who study climate change, and not focus on her or the classes she has skipped. That is not the point.

With the high profile she has achieved, Greta is also committed to giving the world a better understanding of Asperger's syndrome. People like her who live with Asperger's are less inclined to make new friends, get to know people and make small talk, but they can be very talented. And Greta has shown this. Now it is up to us to show we are up to her challenge.

EXPLAINING GLOBAL WARMING TO CHILDREN

Modern life is very different to the way our ancestors lived. Even just a few generations ago, the grandparents of our grandparents lived in a world we would struggle to recognise. Cars to drive around in, heating systems to warm our houses in winter, electrical appliances to help us do our work, and aeroplanes that allow us to travel quickly to faraway countries are all recent "novelties". In the last two hundred years in particular, there have been rapid changes in the way we live. New technology has completely revolutionised our lives.

However, many modern habits are only possible because we burn fossil fuels: for example, petrol (which powers the engines of cars that we use to get around every day), coal (which is burned in power stations and turned into electricity to run our washing machines and other appliances) or natural gas (which is taken from below the ground and used to warm our houses). To live the way we do today, we burn a lot of fuel, even if we don't realise it, because it's happening in the engines of our cars, hidden under the hoods, or in power stations far from the cities where we live.

But burning fuel has a side effect. It releases into the atmosphere what the scientists call greenhouse gases. The most "famous" of these is carbon dioxide. Gases like this end up in the air, high over our heads. They rise into the sky and there they stop and gather. They let through the sun's rays but trap its heat.

The earth's atmosphere naturally creates what scientists have called the "greenhouse effect": it captures some of the sun's heat so that life can exist on our planet. The problem is when polluting gases build up and the greenhouse effect is altered.

Temperatures rise slowly, year after year. It gets warmer even though it is difficult to notice it in everyday life because it is a slow, gradual increase. Scientists record temperatures around the world very accurately. It's the scientists who have alerted us that the consequences of these changes can be very serious.

We have already seen some early warnings of impending disaster: perennial ice is melting, sea levels are rising, and the climate is becoming more and more unpredictable. There are areas where it has stopped raining and others where storms and hurricanes occur more frequently.

It's a very complicated phenomenon. It's

hard to predict precisely what will happen, despite the fact that scientists are monitoring the situation continuously. What is certain is that a lot of them are telling us it's important to reduce greenhouse gas emissions and limit global warming as much as possible.

WHAT CAN WE DO?

Global warming is a very complex phenomenon that even experts have difficulty understanding completely. However, the majority of scientists agree that limiting carbon dioxide and greenhouse gas emissions into the atmosphere is the solution for slowing the warming of the planet. Cutting emissions requires radical decisions and changes, and this is why Greta Thunberg started a protest outside her country's parliament. But every day, each one of us can choose to change the habits that most threaten the health of our planet.

1. Reduce your use of cars as much as possible. The most environmentally friendly ways to get around are to walk or to catch public transport. A bus carrying fifty passengers releases less pollution than a car carrying only two.

2. If you have to use a car, arrange to travel in a group, especially if you have friends who need to go where you are going.

3. Remember to switch off the lights when you leave a room. The electricity that powers the light bulbs in your house is probably produced by burning fossil fuels.

4. Heating water produces pollution: use hot water only when really necessary, making sure you don't waste any.

5. Have a shower instead of a bath: it's a simple way to save on electricity needed to heat the water.

6. Packaging, boxes and wrapping pollute the environment and require energy to make. Whenever you are buying something, examine it carefully. The less packaging it comes in, the better!

7. Choose seasonal vegetables and fruit. The out-of-season fruit in the shops has probably been grown in countries or regions faraway and been shipped to you.

8. Before buying something new, ask yourself if you really need it.

9. Don't overdo the heating in winter: turn it down a degree or two and wear warm layers in the house.

10. In summer, use the air conditioning as little as possible: cooling the air requires electricity.

11. Remember that the electricity you use is produced by burning fuel and releasing carbon dioxide into the atmosphere: use less electricity wherever possible.

Glossary

atmosphere

All around our planet, high above us, is a layer of gas. It completely surrounds the earth and is 1000 kilometres thick. In the part closest to the ground is the air that we breathe, the rain, the snow, the clouds that gather and the weather phenomena we are all familiar with. If the atmosphere were different – or if there wasn't any atmosphere – life on our planet could not exist.

carbon footprint

The amount of carbon dioxide released into the atmosphere by a person, a country, air travel, factories, etc.

climate march

When many people protest publicly, demanding that action be taken to protect the environment.

climate strike

The action taken by Greta Thunberg, protesting against the inaction of people who didn't seem to care about the changes happening all over the world. She started by herself one day in

August 2018, deciding to sit in front of the Swedish Parliament instead of going to school, and soon gained widespread support. Greta is still striking from school every Friday, urging politicians to take serious action to tackle the problem.

CO_2

The scientific term for carbon dioxide, a gas present in the atmosphere.

COP24

The United Nations Climate Conference, 2018. Representatives of almost every country in the world met for two weeks to discuss how to implement the agreement made in Paris just a few years earlier to limit carbon dioxide emissions.

deforestation

The removal of large areas of forest by people. Cutting down trees has serious consequences, because plants help to keep the carbon dioxide levels in the air under control and therefore slow global warming.

electricity

What makes most things in our houses work: we turn on our lights and run our electrical appliances using electricity. Every day factories use electricity to churn out the hundreds of objects all around us. The problem is that electricity is often produced by burning fuel and releasing greenhouse gases into the environment.

environmental activists

People who are committed to protecting the environment, by organising rallies, protesting or distributing information.

environmentalism

The movement of people committed to protecting the environment we live in.

fossil fuel

A particular type of fuel formed over millions of years from a build-up of buried prehistoric animal and vegetable matter. Over many, many years this matter decomposed and turned into oil, natural gas and coal.

Fridays for Future

The Fridays when students all over the world skip classes in order to protest. They want to protect the earth and ensure a dignified future for themselves and generations to come.

fuel
Something that burns to produce energy.

global warming
The slow increase in temperature on our planet over the past 100 years. It is referred to as "global" warming because this pattern has been recorded all over the world, although it's worse in some places than others. Scientists estimate that in the past 100 years the average temperature has increased by 0.75°C.

greenhouse effect

When our atmosphere stores some of the heat produced by the sun, creating the climate we are all familiar with. Human beings only started to understand what was going on high above their heads in the early 1800s, when scientists realised there was "something" in the sky that was filtering the sun's rays.

greenhouse gases

The gases present in the earth's atmosphere that allow the sun's rays to pass through and store some of its heat.

Nobel Prize

The prestigious prize awarded every year to a worthy individual or group of people. Greta was nominated for the

2019 Nobel Peace Prize in recognition of her protesting that if global warming is not stopped this could lead to tragedy for all of humanity.

parliament

Where you will find parliamentarians. These are the people elected by voters to govern a country. The most important decisions on every issue, decisions that affect everyone's wellbeing, are made in a parliament.

perennial ice

These are the ice caps that do not melt even in spring and summer. Most perennial ice caps on the planet are in Greenland and Antarctica.

Riksdag

The Swedish Parliament, situated in Stockholm. It is where Greta decided to protest, demanding action against global warming.

rising sea levels

The result of melting ice, rising sea levels have serious consequences. Scientists believe that large areas of the earth where people currently live will one day be under water.

United Nations

An organisation of 193 countries (almost the entire world!) committed to cooperating to ensure peace and fix disputes without using violence. Their aim is to develop and maintain friendly relationships between countries and promote human rights.

TED (Technology, Entertainment, Design)

Politicians, scientists and brilliant speakers who excel in a variety of subjects walk onto the TED stage to speak about their area of expertise. TED talks follow a philosophy that is clearly spelt out in their slogan: 'ideas worth spreading'.

Timeline

Important dates in the history of human pollution and global warming

1765 Scottish engineer James Watt improves on the steam engine first developed by Thomas Newcomen in 1712, finding a way to turn steam into movement. It is one of the inventions that leads to the Industrial Revolution, one of the most radical transformations in the way people live. Machines start to do our work for us, but more quickly and efficiently. Suddenly it is possible to make a lot of things with very little effort. The problem is that the machines operate by burning coal.

With the Industrial Revolution, problems caused by environmental pollution also begin.

1824 The physicist Jean-Baptiste-Joseph Fourier works out that high up in the sky above us there is a layer of gas capable of capturing the heat of the sun.

1883 Car factories are built in several European countries. Cars are big, unreliable and very slow, travelling at barely more than 50 kilometres per hour. At the time it is hard to imagine how many cars there will be on the roads in every country just one hundred years later, releasing carbon dioxide into the atmosphere.

1952 In December, London endures the catastrophic results of uncontrolled pollution. The air becomes heavy, grey and smelly, and smog fills the city. The situation is so bad that you can only see a few metres in front of you. It becomes impossible to drive. Public transport comes to a halt and schools close. People's health suffers enormously, and for the first time the English have to think seriously about the consequences of air pollution.

1972 The first political party whose priority is to protect the environment, called the Australian Greens, is founded in Tasmania, Australia.

1973 The idea of a "green" political party becomes popular. The English copy the Australians and the PEOPLE Party is born.

1979 By now, scientists have realised that the climate is changing, and politicians organise the first world conference to discuss the subject.

1997 The representatives of many countries meet in Kyoto, Japan, to discuss environmental issues. They sign an agreement in which they commit to reduce pollution released into the atmosphere. There were many other meetings before and after Kyoto and as time has gone by the need for real action has become more urgent.

2015 After many years of talking about climate problems, the representatives of many countries meet in Paris to decide how to tackle the climate emergency. They agree to limit the increase in temperature to well below 2°C.

2018 On the 20th of August, Greta Thunberg decides to skip school and protest outside the Swedish Parliament.

Are You Interested in This Issue? Here's Some Further Reading

1. Jonathan Watts, "Greta Thunberg, schoolgirl climate change warrior: 'Some people can let things go. I can't'", *The Guardian* (online), 11 March 2019, www.theguardian.com/world/2019/mar/11/greta-thunberg-schoolgirl-climate-change-warrior-some-people-can-let-things-go-i-cant

2. Damian Carrington, "'Our leaders are like children,' school strike founder tells climate summit", *The Guardian* (online), 4 December 2018, www.theguardian.com/environment/2018/dec/04/leaders-like-children-school-strike-founder-greta-thunberg-tells-un-climate-summit

3. Masha Gessen, "A fifteen-year-old climate activist who is demanding a new kind of politics", *The New Yorker* (online), 2 October 2018, www.newyorker.com/news/our-columnists/ the-fifteen-year-old-climate-activist-who-is- demanding-a-new-kind-of-politics

4. "Climate crusading schoolgirl Greta Thunberg pleads next generation's case", *The Straits Times* (online), 5 December 2018, www.straitstimes.com/ world/europe/climate-crusading-schoolgirl-greta-thunberg- pleads-next-generations-case

5. Damian Carrington, "Greta Thunberg nominated for Nobel Peace Prize", *The Guardian* (online), 14 March 2019, www.theguardian.com/world/2019/ mar/14/greta-thunberg-nominated-nobel-peace-prize

6. Greta Thunberg, "Why I began the climate protests that are going global", *New Scientist*, 13 March 2019, www.newscientist.com/article/mg24132213-400-greta-thunberg-why-i-began-the-climate-protests-that-are-going- global/

7. Greta Thunberg, "I'm striking from school to protest inaction on climate change – you should too", *The Guardian* (online), 26 November 2018, www.theguardian.com/commentisfree/2018/nov/26/im-striking-from-school-for-climate-change-too-save-the-world-australians-students-should-too

8. Andrea Germanos, "'This is our darkest hour': With declaration of rebellion, new group vows mass civil disobedience to save planet", *commondreams.org*, 31 October 2018, www.commondreams.org/news/2018/10/31/our-darkest-hour-declaration-rebellion-new-group-vows-mass-civil-disobedience-save